Transportation & Communication Series

Police and Emergency Vehicles

Arlene Bourgeois Molzahn

Enslow Publishers, Inc.

40 Industrial Road   PO Box 38
Box 398   Aldershot
Berkeley Heights, NJ 07922   Hants GU12 6BP
USA   UK

http://www.enslow.com

To my grandson, Michael, whose smile lights up my life and to D.A.R.E. Officer Van who helps so many children.

Copyright © 2002 by Enslow Publishers, Inc.

Library of Congress Cataloging-in-Publication Data

Molzahn, Arlene Bourgeois.
    Police and emergency vehicles / Arlene Bourgeois Molzahn.
       p. cm. — (Transportation & communication series)
    Includes bibliographical references and index.
    Summary: Discusses the history of police and emergency vehicles, how they are used, and the future of these helpful and lifesaving vehicles.
    ISBN 0-7660-1890-3
    1. Police vehicles—Juvenile literature. 2. Emergency vehicles—Juvenile literature. [1. Police vehicles. 2. Emergency vehicles.] I. Title. II. Series.
HV7936.V4 M65 2002
629.225—dc21   2001005852

Printed in the United States of America

10 9 8 7 6 5 4 3 2 1

Illustration Credits: Star-Ledger photo by Chris Barth, p. 40; Sean F. Cassidy, p. 30; Corel Corporation, pp. 4, 7 (top), 8, 9, 10, 14 (bottom), 17 (top), 18, 26, 34 (bottom), 35 (bottom), 41 (bottom), 42; Dover Publications, Inc., p. 22; Tim Farrell/The Star-Ledger, p. 37 (bottom); Hemera Technologies, Inc. 1997-2000, pp. 1, 2, 5, 6, 7 (bottom), 11, 12 (top), 16 (top), 17 (bottom), 19, 20 (bottom), 27, 33, 35 (top), 36 (bottom), 37 (top), 39, 41 (top); Steve Klaver/The Star-Ledger, p. 29 (bottom); Tony Kurdzuk/The Star-Ledger, p. 15; Star-Ledger photo by Phil Lanoue, p. 13 (bottom); Library of Congress, pp. 20 (top), 21; Jerry McCrea/The Star-Ledger, p. 13 (top, inset); Courtesy of the Morris County (NJ) Sheriff's Office, pp. 28, 34 (top); National Archives, p. 24; Courtesy of Odyssey Automotive Specialty, p. 12 (bottom); William Perlman/The Star-Ledger, p. 14 (top, inset); Courtesy of Township of Roxbury, N.J. Police Community Service Unit, p. 32; Courtesy of Sikorsky Aircraft Corp./Rich Zellner, pp. 16 (bottom), 23, 25, 31, 36 (top), 43; Star-Ledger photo by Jim Wright, pp. 29 (top), 38.

Cover Illustration: Courtesy of Sikorsky Aircraft Corp./Rich Zellner.

Contents

Chapter 1

Missing Children

At four o'clock in the afternoon a call was made to 911. The caller, Joe Jenkins, said that his family was camping at Sunrise Campgrounds. He reported that his two children were missing.

The 911 operator called police headquarters. Two police officers on patrol were radioed about the missing children. They quickly set off for the campground. The police officers wanted the children to get medical help as soon as they were found. So an ambulance was also sent to the campground.

Mr. and Mrs. Jenkins looked all over for their children.

5

When the first police officer arrived at the campgrounds, he talked to Mr. and Mrs. Jenkins. They said that their three-year-old daughter, Clare, was wearing a yellow top and blue shorts. Their four-year-old son, Troy, was wearing a red shirt and blue shorts.

After lunch, the family had gone for a short walk. When they returned, they all took a nap in their tent. When Mr. and Mrs. Jenkins woke up, Clare and Troy were not in the tent. Mr. and Mrs. Jenkins quickly began looking for them. But they could not find them. Word of the missing children soon spread. Everyone began looking and calling for them. But there was no sign of the children.

When the second police officer arrived, the campground was divided into two parts. One police officer was put in charge of each part. Volunteers

from the campgrounds helped look for the children. The groups kept in touch by cell phone.

By nine o'clock that night, the children had not been found. It was too dark to continue the search.

The next morning, the police called for a helicopter to help with the search. They also called for a K-9 unit with a police dog. The local radio and television stations were called. They let people know that volunteers were needed to search for the missing children.

These people are on a canoeing camping trip.

The search began to spread outside of the campground. Shortly after ten o'clock, the helicopter crew radioed that they had spotted something red. It was in some tall grass about three miles from the campground. It was about a block from the road. The search teams were called.

Everyone hurried to that area. They found the children sitting in the grass. Both were scared, hungry, and covered with mosquito

The search parties finally found the children in some tall grass.

These people are helping a person who fell.

bites. The ambulance took them to the hospital where doctors said they would be fine.

Everyone who had helped in the search was very happy to hear the news. Mr. and Mrs. Jenkins and their children were very happy, too. They thanked everyone for doing a great job. By the afternoon the family was back at the campground.

Chapter 2

Police and Emergency Vehicles

Police cars are found in all police departments in the United States. They are found in nearly every police department in the world.

Police need cars that can go very fast. They must be able to catch people who break the law. They need to answer emergency calls quickly. They need to hurry to help people who have had an accident. Police also hurry to help fire departments when there is a fire. They direct traffic away from the fire.

Some police units may use cars like this (left). It used to be an armored-car.

This picture shows the inside of an emergency vehicle. There are siren controls and radios.

When a police car is hurrying to an emergency, it uses its siren. The screeching siren whistle tells everyone to get out of the way. Police cars have a row of lights on the roof. These lights can be red, blue, and white. Some emergency lights can also be yellow or green. When these lights are turned on they keep flashing. This is another way police tell everyone to keep out of the way.

Police vehicles are equipped with two-way radios. People at the police station use a radio to tell police officers where they are needed.

Sometimes a police officer cannot take care of an emergency alone. Then the officer uses the radio to call for help.

Many police vehicles are equipped with computers. The computers are used by police to check for stolen cars. Computers also help find people who are wanted by the police.

Police officers use bicycles in places where it would be hard to go with a police car. They are used where large groups of people have

Police officers can also use bicycles to patrol streets or use them where cars might not be able to go.

Motorcycles are another way police officers can patrol streets.

gathered. Many times police officers patrol concerts, fairs, and large picnics on bicycles.

Motorcycles are another special type of police vehicle. They are often used for crowd control. Motorcycles are equipped with two-way radios and computers just like police cars. They have a siren and a flashing emergency light. They can reach trouble spots faster than bicycles. In warm weather, motorcycles are sometimes used to patrol streets. They are cheaper to buy and cheaper to operate than police cars.

The United States Coast Guard is a

branch of the armed services. Its ships patrol the coast of the United States and the Great Lakes. The Coast Guard is always ready for emergencies on the water. The Coast Guard helps rescue people who have been in boating accidents. Boats that have broken down at sea are towed to shore by the Coast Guard.

Emergency Medical Technicians, or EMTs,

Some police departments use horses while on patrol.

are people who are trained to take care of sick or hurt people. The EMTs on the rescue ships give aid to the people that they rescue. Coast Guard helicopters fly people who are badly hurt to hospitals on shore.

Helicopters and airplanes are used by police to catch speeders on busy highways. They are used to search wooded and hilly areas for lost people. Helicopters can land on very small clearings. They can rescue people in places

The United States Coast Guard is always ready for emergencies.

that other vehicles cannot reach. People who are very sick or badly hurt are flown to hospitals in helicopters. EMTs in the helicopters care for the patients until they reach the hospitals.

This is a view from the inside of a helicopter.

Ambulances are like trucks with emergency care and life support equipment. They have a siren and flashing emergency lights like a police vehicle. Ambulances can travel very fast. They take sick or hurt people to hospitals. EMTs in the ambulances can talk on a two-way radio to the doctors at the hospital. The doctors help the EMTs decide what kind of emergency healthcare the patient needs.

A rescue vehicle that is important to keep highways safe is the tow truck. It helps to quickly remove wrecked or broken down cars that are on the highway. This helps stop traffic jams from happening. It helps to keep traffic moving smoothly.

Chapter 3

Vehicles of Long Ago

Police Cars

Police departments did not always have cars. Before cars were invented, police officers on duty walked the city streets. In busy areas of the city, policemen rode horses. They hurried to emergencies on horseback. The first police vehicles were wagons pulled by horses.

The first police car used in the United States was in 1899 in Akron, Ohio. It was an electric car that was powered by batteries. It could travel at a speed of 16 miles per hour.

There was not a great need for police cars until people began buying automobiles.

In busy areas of some cities, police officers ride horses (left).

In 1908, the Ford Motor Company began to build the Model T Ford. This car was built for the average family in the United States. It was priced low enough so that many families could buy one. Fifteen million Model T Ford cars had been sold by 1927.

With so many cars on the roads, police departments also needed cars. Until the mid-1950s, police cars were nearly all made by the Ford Motor Company. These cars had a siren and flashing emergency lights. But they did not have special engines. So they could not go faster than other cars.

Rescue Vehicles

In 1487, during a war in Spain, rescue vehicles were used for the first time to bring hurt soldiers to hospitals. They were large open wooden wagons pulled by horses.

In the 1920s, police officers chased down this car.

Baron Dominique-Jean Larrey, a French army doctor, made the first ambulance in 1792. It was a small covered cart pulled by horses. It was first used during wartime to bring hurt soldiers to hospitals.

In 1869, Bellevue Hospital in New York City started using horse-drawn ambulances. In 1908, ambulances were built on car frames and they had engines. Horses were no longer needed.

The photo below was taken in the late 1880s. It shows an ambulance traveling with a wagon train. The ambulance is the wagon with the Red Cross flag. The top photo is an ambulance from the 1920s.

Helicopters

Leonardo da Vinci was an artist and a scientist who lived in Italy. In the year 1483, he drew up plans for a helicopter but he never built it. In 1784, two Frenchmen, Launoy and Bienvenu, made a model helicopter that could fly. Many other people experimented with building helicopters. But no one built a helicopter that could stay in the air for more than a few minutes.

Then in 1936, Henrich Focke built a helicopter that could fly for one hour and 20 minutes. It could go 76 miles per hour. But it was very hard to control in the air. A Russian-born American, Igor Sikorsky, built the first helicopter that really worked. In 1934, the United Aircraft Corporation gave Sikorsky $30,000 to build a helicopter. By 1939, Sikorsky had built a helicopter that could fly. It did not look like the helicopters of today. The pilot sat on a seat in the open air.

Leonardo da Vinci (above) and a sketch of his helicopter (below).

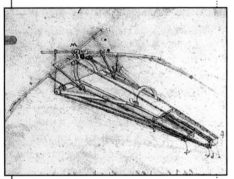

Igor Sikorsky tries out his helicopter (right).

World War II lasted from 1939 to 1945. Germany, Italy, and Japan were at war with many other countries in the world. The German troops had captured many countries in Europe. By 1941, helicopters were used to fly over enemy lines. They could land behind enemy lines and rescue airplane crews whose airplanes had been shot down. Then they

Helicopters were used during the Korean War to get injured soldiers to mobile hospitals.

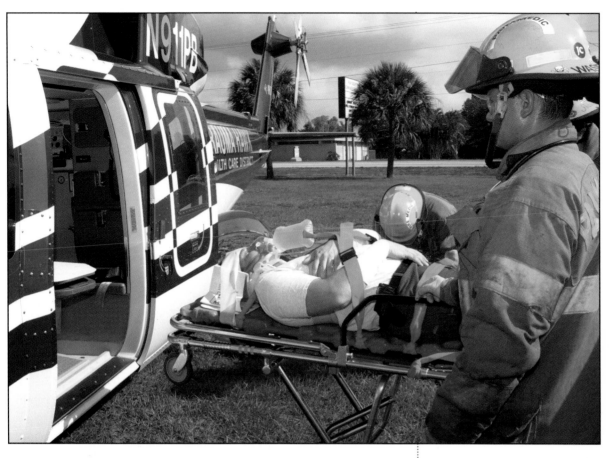

Rescue helicopters can fly a person who is badly hurt to a hospital.

would be safely returned to their bases. From 1965 to 1973, the United States was at war in Vietnam. Helicopters saved many more lives during that war. In 1991, helicopters were also used in the Persian Gulf War. Many peacetime uses were also found for helicopters.

Making Better Vehicles

Over the years better police and rescue vehicles have been made.

In the 1950s, car companies began making special cars for police. They called these cars "police packages." Both the General Motors Company and the Ford Motor Company made special cars for police departments. They had improved brakes and powerful engines that could travel much faster than other cars. Nearly every car manufacturer today makes a "police package."

Police vehicles carry a lot of equipment. They carry computers, radar guns, video

Helicopters can land in the middle of highways. (left). This crew is helping a person who was rescued from a cliff.

Some police departments have special K-9 units with dogs specially trained to help police officers. Some dogs are trained to find bombs (bottom). The trailer is a safe way to transport explosives.

cameras, handcuffs, flares, first aid kits, and pepper spray. The equipment they carry is used to control people who break the law. Some police departments have Sport Utility Vehicles (SUVs) that are made to carry specially trained dogs. These units are called K-9 units.

The improvements in police cars have helped to make the lives of people safer. Police can get to emergencies quickly. They can keep dangerous drivers off the streets, and they can control traffic. Better police cars make law enforcement easier and safer for police officers.

Ambulances of today are very different from the

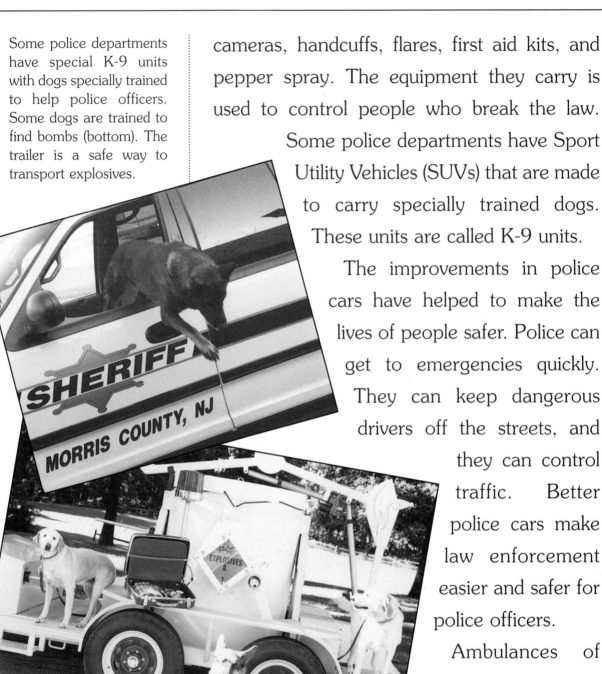

ones of long ago. Until the 1970s, ambulances just carried very sick or hurt people to hospitals. There was very little emergency healthcare equipment in them. The vehicles were so small there was no room for anyone to give medical treatment to a patient.

Today's ambulances are like hospitals on wheels. Some ambulances have two EMTs in them. They carry first aid supplies. They have oxygen for people who are having trouble breathing. They also carry equipment to help someone who has had a heart attack. Two-way radios make it possible for EMTs to talk to doctors at the hospital. The doctors can tell the EMTs what

Police cars have many things that help police officers. This monitor shows what happens while a police officer is talking to a driver.

This police officer is holding a radar gun. Radar guns can help police officers catch people who are speeding.

to do for the patient. EMTs in ambulances have saved thousands of lives.

Helicopters have changed greatly since the first one made by the United Aircraft Corporation. Pilots no longer sit in the open air like Igor Sikorsky had to do. The Bell Aircraft Company was one of the first to begin working to make helicopters better. In 1943,

Ambulances are like hospitals on wheels. EMTs in ambulances help save many lives.

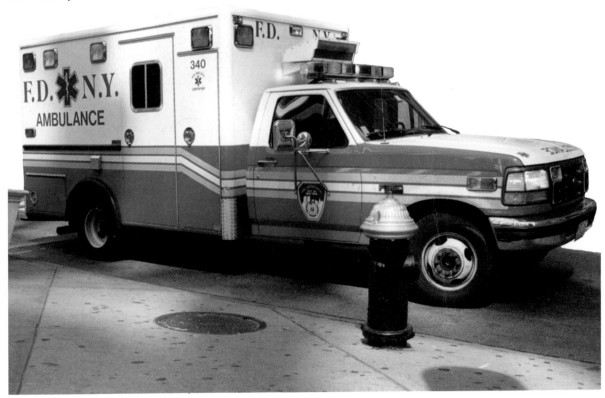

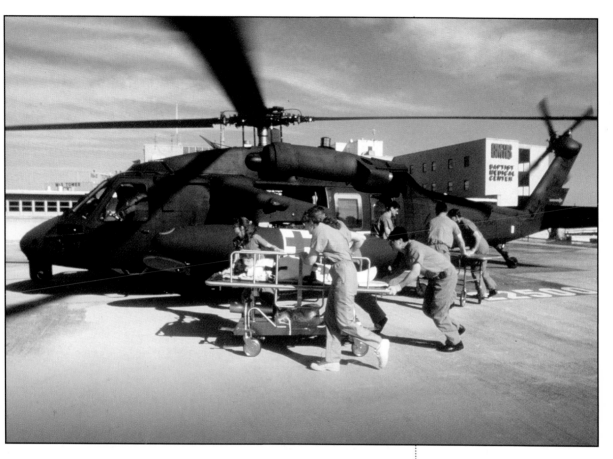

better rotor systems on helicopters were made.

Rescue helicopters are really flying ambulances. They fly very sick or hurt people to hospitals in cities far away. They have emergency equipment in them and EMTs who know how to use the equipment. Helicopters have become very important.

This crew is rushing a patient to a helicopter. Helicopters can fly quickly to hospitals.

Chapter 5

All Types of Jobs

Years ago only men were police officers and rescue workers. Today women and men work side by side on all these jobs.

Police departments have many special types of cars. Most police cars are patrol cars. Police officers drive these cars around and answer emergency calls. Many places have a Drug Abuse Resistance Education (D.A.R.E.) program where police officers teach children to keep away from drugs. Those police officers have specially painted cars with "D.A.R.E." painted on them.

Police dogs are trained to help police

D.A.R.E. officers use special cars. Some might look like this (left).

officers find people who are lost. They also are used to search for drugs. They help control groups of people who disobey the laws. Dogs are a very important part of many big city police departments. Most big cities have a few special cars that are made to carry police dogs. Many people have jobs in car factories to make the special types of cars police departments need. Other people have jobs training dogs for the police.

It takes many different workers to make the equipment needed in police vehicles. Workers in factories make sirens and special lights for police cars. Other factory workers make radios, telephones, computers, and video cameras that are used by police.

Police departments have special units that use tear gas to control groups that are not

Dogs that are specially trained are a big help to police officers.

following the law. Workers in chemical factories are needed to make tear gas.

Police cars have radar guns in them. Police officers check the speed of a car by using a radar gun.

Police cars carry regular guns that shoot bullets. They are carried in a safe way and are used only when necessary. People working in factories make different kinds of guns for the police.

These EMTs and fire fighters are helping a person who was hurt in an accident.

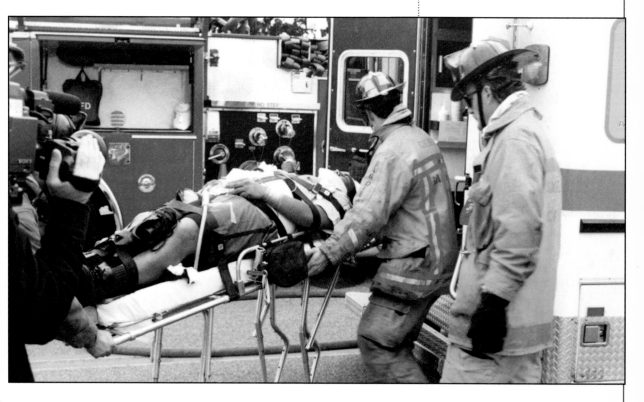

Many people are needed to make emergency vehicles. These people are working on a helicopter.

Ambulances are one of the most used rescue vehicles. They are used to rush thousands of people to hospitals each day. Factory workers are needed to make ambulances. Workers in other factories make the medical supplies that are used in an ambulance.

Police departments use many computers. They hire people who are trained to use computers. They also need computer technicians to keep all the computers running.

Police departments hire people to answer 911 calls. These people must be trained to do their jobs well. They need to be good listeners. They need to know where to send the emergency vehicles. They need to know what kind of vehicles to send. Many people work to help the police when there is an emergency.

Some people have jobs making special helicopters. Other workers make the rescue equipment helicopters carry.

Police departments need people who are good listeners to answer 911 calls.

Chapter 6

Newer, Better, Safer

Police vehicles will always be needed to help keep us safe. Police departments want vehicles that will help police officers do their jobs well. They look for a few things when they buy new vehicles. They want vehicles that are easy to drive, have powerful engines and good brakes. The safety of police officers is very important. It is thought about when buying police vehicles.

The police car that the Ford Motor Company makes today is the Intercepter model of the Crown Victoria Ford. The Ford Motor Company is planning on making a new

Here is a view from the driver's seat in a police car (left).

This police officer is watching a video monitor from his car.

police package soon. General Motors has a Chevrolet Impala car that is made for police use.

Police officers depend on good communication. Much work has been done to improve ways to communicate between police cars and police headquarters. Work is also being done to improve communication between police cars.

New ways are being used to control crowds

of people. New equipment for controlling large groups is being placed in police cars. Special guns have been invented that shoot an electric shock. The electric shock stops the lawbreaker. It does not permanently hurt the person. It knocks the lawbreaker down. This gives the police time to handcuff the person. This new type of gun is called a TASER®. Soon TASERs may be found in all police vehicles.

Police officers need to be trained in how to arrest people who have broken the law.

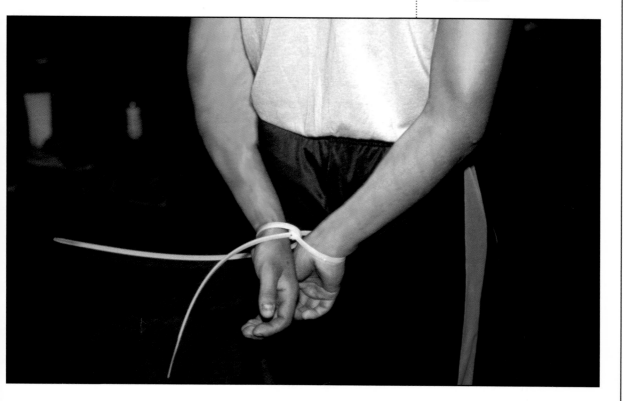

Ambulances will continue to be important rescue vehicles. Engineers are working to make ambulances safer as they speed to help sick and hurt people. More and more medical devices are being put in ambulances. These will improve the aid that EMTs give to people.

Engineers are always looking for ways to make helicopters safer and faster. They are working to improve the jet engines that are used in helicopters.

Some parts of the helicopter are being made with a new type of plastic. These plastic parts make the helicopter lighter. Lighter and more powerful engines give the helicopter more speed. Speed for helicopters is important. Very sick or hurt people need to get to hospitals as quickly as possible. Speed is also important when

Many people become police officers.

helicopters are used to search for people who are lost. It is not good for someone to go for a long time without food or water. So, it is important to find a lost person quickly. One of the newest helicopters can fly as fast as 345 miles per hour.

More powerful engines also help the helicopter to fly higher and to carry heavier loads. These engines also help to better control the helicopter in windy weather. Plastic parts also make the helicopters last longer.

Police vehicles, ambulances, helicopters, rescue boats, and tow trucks help make our lives better and safer.

The faster the helicopter travels, the quicker it can reach a lost or hurt person.

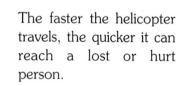

Timeline

1483—Leonardo da Vinci draws plans for a helicopter.

1487—Open wagons pulled by horses are used to rescue soldiers on the battlefields.

1792—Baron Dominique-Jean Larrey builds the first covered ambulance.

1869—Bellevue Hospital in New York City begins to use horse-drawn ambulances.

1899—The first electric-powered police car is used in the United States.

1908—Ambulances are built on car frames and are run by gasoline engines; Ford Motor Company begins to build the Model T Ford car.

1939—Igor Sikorsky builds the first helicopter that really could fly.

1950—Car companies begin to work on special cars called police packages for police departments.

2001—Better police vehicles, ambulances, and helicopters are made.

Words to Know

accident—Something that is not planned but that usually happens because of a mistake.

ambulance—A rescue vehicle used to take hurt or sick people to a hospital.

communicate—To share or pass along feelings, thoughts, or information.

emergency—A sudden need for help.

Emergency Medical Technician (EMT)—A person who is trained to take care of hurt or sick people before they can get to a hospital.

equipment—Tools that people use to do their jobs.

patient—Someone who needs medical care.

rescue—To save from danger or harm.

siren—A kind of horn that makes a loud screeching sound.

Learn More About
Police and Emergency Vehicles

Books

Freeman, Marcia S. *Police Cars*. Mankato, MN: Capstone Press, 1999.

Greene, Carol. *At the Police Station*. Eden Prairie, MN: Child's World, Inc., 1997.

Greene, Carol. *Police Officers Protect People*. Eden Prairie, MN: Child's World, Inc., 1997.

Kelly, Zachary A. *Law Enforcement*. Vero Beach, FL: The Rourke Corporation, Inc., 1999.

Ready, Dee. *Police Officers*. Mankato, MN: Capstone Press, 1997.

Rogers, Hal. *Ambulances*. Eden Prairie, MN: The Child's World, Inc., 2000.

Rogers, Hal. *Rescue Helicopters*. Eden Prairie, MN: The Child's World, Inc., 2000.

Stille, Darlene R. *Helicopters*. New York: Children's Press, 1997.

Learn More About
Police and Emergency Vehicles

Internet Addresses

Ambulance History

<http://inventors.about.com/library/inventors/blambulance.htm>

Learn more about the history of ambulances.

City of Santa Monica: Inside Our Police Cars

<http://santamonicapd.org/information/interior.htm>

Find out what the inside of a police car looks like from this Web site from the Santa Monica (California) Police Department.

Index